Explore Outer Space

NEBULAE

by Ruth Owen

WINDMILL
BOOKS

New York

Published in 2013 by Windmill Books, An Imprint of Rosen Publishing
29 East 21st Street, New York, NY 10010

Produced for Windmill by Ruby Tuesday Books Ltd
Editor for Ruby Tuesday Books Ltd: Mark J. Sachner
US Editor: Sara Antill
Designer: Emma Randall
Consultant: Kevin Yates, Space Communications Manager, National Space Centre, Leicester, United Kingdom

Photo Credits:
Cover, 26–27 © Shutterstock; 1, 15 © Marco Burali, Tiziano Capecchi, Marco Mancini (Osservatorio MTM); 2, 3, 4, 7, 11, 12–13, 14, 16–17, 19, 20, 21, 22–23, 24–25, © Hubble Space Telescope, NASA and ESA; 8–9 © ESO/INAF-VST/OmegaCAM. Acknowledgement: OmegaCen/Astro-WISE/Kapteyn Institute; 10 © Chesnok/Wikipedia Creative Commons (Public Domain); 18 © NASA/ESA/AURA/Caltech; 28–29 © European Southern Observatory (ESO).

Library of Congress Cataloging-in-Publication Data

Owen, Ruth. 1967–
Nebulae / by Ruth Owen.
    p. cm. — (Explore outer space)
Includes index.
ISBN 978-1-4488-8075-1 (library binding) — ISBN 978-1-4488-8117-8 (pbk.) — ISBN 978-1-4488-8122-2 (6-pack)
1. Nebulae—Juvenile literature. I. Title.
QB855.2.O94 2011
523.1'135—dc23

2012000172

Manufactured in the United States of America

CPSIA Compliance Information: Batch # B3S12WM: For Further Information contact Windmill Books, New York, New York at 1-866-478-0556

CONTENTS

Beautiful Nebulae 4

The Life and Death of Stars 6

Measuring Nebulae 8

Star Factories 10

The Orion Nebula 12

Dark Nebulae 14

Cool, Blue Reflection Nebulae 16

Reflection Nebulae in Action 18

Planetary Nebulae 20

Supernovas 22

The Crab Nebula 24

A Very Important Nebula 26

Recycling Stars 28

Glossary 30

Websites 31

Read More, Index 32

Beautiful Nebulae

A giant, towerlike column stretches upward—just like something in a story about a fantasy kingdom. Is this tower the hiding place of an evil wizard? Is it some ancient, magical structure on a mountaintop?

No! The tower is a column of gas, 57 trillion miles (92 trillion km) high. It's floating in space, trillions and trillions of miles (km) from Earth. The incredible gas tower is part of the Eagle **Nebula**.

The word "nebula" is the Latin word for "cloud." Nebulas, or nebulae, are vast clouds of gas and dust. They are the places where stars begin their lives, and many are formed from the matter that is left behind when stars die.

Nebulae form in many different sizes, shapes, and colors. Like beautiful fantasy worlds, these clouds are quite possibly the most amazing sights in space!

This giant tower-shaped cloud of cold gas and dust is part of the Eagle Nebula.

That's Out of This World!

Many of the incredible images of nebulae in this book were obtained by the **Hubble Space Telescope**. Hubble **orbits** Earth outside of our **atmosphere**. Unlike telescopes on Earth, Hubble can detect distant objects in space more clearly because the gases in our atmosphere do not blur its view.

Nebula NGC 604 is a place where stars are born. At its center are over 200 stars up to 60 times bigger than our Sun!

THE LIFE AND DEATH OF STARS

To understand how different types of nebulae form, and what happens inside some nebulae, it's helpful to know about the life cycles of stars.

Stars form inside some types of nebulae. When dust and gas in these nebulae begin to shrink under their own **gravity**, they break into clumps. The shrinking clumps of gas and dust get hotter and hotter until they ignite into burning balls of gas—stars!

A star like our Sun "lives" by burning its gases for billions of years. Eventually, the star will use up all its fuel, and its life will come to an end. These stars die slowly over millions of years. As they fade, they gradually eject their outer layers, forming a nebula.

Other more massive stars die suddenly in a huge explosion called a **supernova**. As a star explodes, a vast gas cloud spreads out into space. This cloud is also a nebula.

A new young star in the Orion Nebula surrounded by the remains of the cloud from which it formed

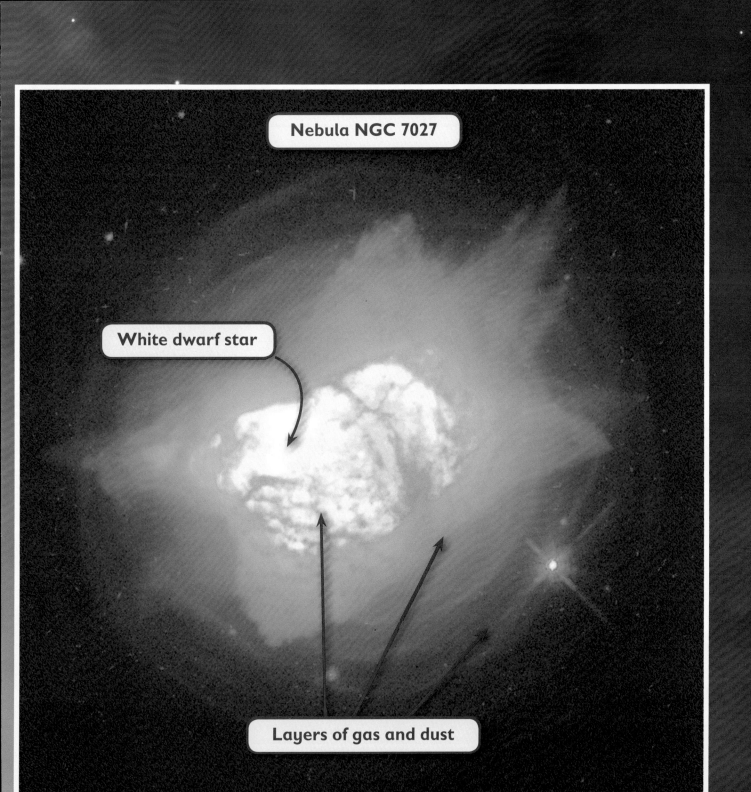

Nebula NGC 7027

White dwarf star

Layers of gas and dust

That's Out of This World!

The Hubble Telescope's image of nebula NGC 7027 shows the death of a star. The star has ejected its outer layers of gas and dust. All that remains of the star is a small, hot core known as a **white dwarf** star.

MEASURING NEBULAE

When we drive to another state or fly to another country, we measure the distance in miles or kilometers. We can even use miles when measuring distances in our **solar system.** The Sun, for example, is about 93 million miles (149.7 million km) from Earth. When we study distant space structures such as nebulae, however, the measurements needed are too big to use miles or kilometers.

To measure how far a nebula is from Earth, scientists use a unit of measurement called a **light year.** The fastest thing we know of is light. It travels at about 186,500 miles per second (300,000 km/s). A light year is the distance that light can travel in one year. So, if something is one light year from Earth, it is over 5.8 trillion miles (9.4 trillion km) away.

That's Out of This World!

The closest star-forming nebula to Earth is the Orion Nebula. It is about 1,500 light years from Earth. The Omega Nebula (pictured here) has a diameter of 15 light years. It is between 5,000 and 6,000 light years from Earth.

The Omega Nebula

STAR FACTORIES

Nebulae in which stars form are often called "star factories" or "star nurseries." Their scientific name is diffuse nebulae.

The gases and dust of a diffuse nebula are the ingredients for making new stars. When very hot stars form in a diffuse nebula they heat the gas to the point where it glows pinkish-red. The nebula is then known as an emission nebula.

The Carina Nebula is an emission nebula in our **galaxy**, the **Milky Way**. It is 7,500 light years from Earth. The Chandra X-ray Observatory, a telescope that, like Hubble, orbits Earth, has detected over 14,000 stars in this nebula!

Carina Nebula

That's Out of This World!

The Hubble Telescope image on this page shows a small section of the Carina Nebula. At the top of the pillar-like column are jets of gas. The jets are being blasted into space by a new star that is forming inside the tip of the column.

Jets of gas from a new star

A section of the Carina Nebula

THE ORION NEBULA

In 2006, the world got to see the most detailed image ever of the Orion Nebula—the closest "star factory" to Earth.

The picture was pieced together, like a beautiful jigsaw puzzle, with images collected by the Hubble Telescope during 105 orbits around Earth. The Hubble image shows the entire nebula, which is more than 20 light years in diameter.

Massive stars at the center of the Orion Nebula have blown away much of the dust and gas in which they were formed. This allowed Hubble to get a clear view inside the nebula. The Hubble image showed **astronomers** that the Orion Nebula is home to about 3,000 stars.

The stars inside the Orion Nebula are at different stages in their formation. Hubble's detailed "before, during, and after" images of star formation will help astronomers understand more about the life cycles of stars.

That's Out of This World!

The Hubble image of the Orion Nebula shows new stars still forming in the middle of clumps of gas and dust. It also shows young stars being circled by chunks of material that might one day become planets orbiting a star.

The Hubble Telescope's image of the Orion Nebula

DARK NEBULAE

From a swirling, dark cloud 1,500 light years from Earth, a majestic horse's head rises into space. Once again, this fantastic shape is not some fantasy creature, but simply a horse-shaped cloud of gas and dust—a nebula!

The Horsehead Nebula is a type of nebula known as a dark nebula, or absorption nebula. Dark nebulae are thick clouds of dust that absorb any light that reaches them. In the darkness of space, it can be nearly impossible to see a dark nebula. They can only be seen if there is a bright area of space behind them.

The Horsehead Nebula is visible because its backdrop is a cloud of gas that is being lit up by a star named Sigma Orionis. The horse's head is seen as a silhouette against the background of bright, colorful gas.

That's Out of This World!

In 2001, to celebrate Hubble's eleventh birthday, NASA offered astronomers, teachers, and students the chance to vote online for an object in space for the Hubble Space Telescope to observe. The Horsehead Nebula, with 5,000 votes, was the most popular choice. The image (right) was taken by Hubble.

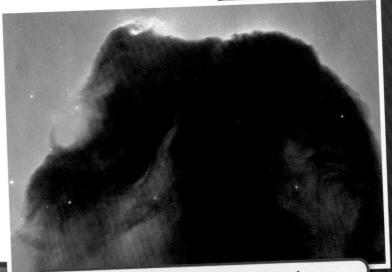

The Hubble Space Telescope image of the Horsehead Nebula in 2001

Horsehead Nebula

COOL, BLUE REFLECTION NEBULAE

Unlike hot, pinkish-red emission nebulae, some nebulae are made up of cool gases and dust. These nebulae, which are bluish-white in color, are called reflection nebulae.

Reflection nebulae do not produce any light of their own. The clouds of dust and gas shine because they reflect the light of a nearby star. It's the same effect as when fog is lit up in the headlights of a car at night. The fog has no light of its own. It is just reflecting the brightness of the car's lights.

Nebula NGC 1999 is a reflection nebula that is lit up by a young star named V380 Orionis. The nebula is made up of gas and dust that was left over when the star formed.

That's Out of This World!

Astronomers estimate that V380 Orionis has a mass that is three and a half times that of our Sun. Its glowing white color comes from a high surface temperature of around 18,000 degrees Fahrenheit (10,000 degrees Celsius). That's double the temperature of the Sun's surface!

**Reflection nebula
NGC 1999**

**Young star
V380 Orionis**

REFLECTION NEBULAE IN ACTION

The **Pleiades** is a cluster, or group, of stars about 425 light years from Earth. Seven of the brightest stars are known as the Seven Sisters. These stars can be seen at night without a telescope. It's also possible to see bluish-white nebulae around the stars!

The bluish cloud around the Seven Sisters is not leftover material from when the stars formed. It is actually a vast cloud of mostly hydrogen gas that is drifting past and among the stars. The cloud is traveling at about 6.8 miles per second (11 km/s).

The cloud cannot be seen on its own. When areas of the cloud get close to a star, however, light from the star reflects off dust particles floating in the gas. This creates a reflection nebula around that star.

The Seven Sisters

These two stars are seen as a single star when viewed from Earth without a telescope.

Merope

The Seven Sisters star Merope is just out of view (top right) in this Hubble Telescope image.

This is the Barnard's Merope Nebula, named after astronomer E. E. Barnard, who discovered the glowing cloud in 1890.

That's Out of This World!

This Hubble Telescope image shows the nebula close to Merope, one of the Seven Sisters stars. Even though the cloud is traveling several miles (km) a second, it will take several thousand years for it to pass Merope.

PLANETARY NEBULAE

When a star like our **Sun** burns up all its gases and begins to die, it grows larger and larger and becomes a **red giant.** Then, the huge star begins to blow off layers of gas and dust into space. These layers from a dying star eventually become a planetary nebula.

Planetary nebulae get their name because they have a round shape, like a planet.

About 5,000 light years from Earth is the Calabash Nebula. Here, material from a dying star is flying out into space at speeds of around 1 million miles an hour (1.6 million km/h)! Astronomers estimate that it will take about 1,000 years for the clouds of gas and dust to form a round-shaped planetary nebula.

The Cat's Eye planetary nebula

White dwarf star

Layers of gas

That's Out of This World!

The Calabash Nebula is also known as the Rotten Egg Nebula because it contains lots of **sulfur**. If we could smell this nebula, the sulfur would give it the smell of rotten eggs!

Calabash, or Rotten Egg, Nebula

Dying star

Material being blown off by the dying star

SUPERNOVAS

Some stars do not die slowly over thousands and thousands of years. Some stars go out with a bang!

Huge stars, over eight times the mass of our Sun, end their lives in a giant explosion called a supernova. As these stars run out of fuel, they expand to become **red supergiants**. Finally, unable to keep burning, they blow apart in a truly massive explosion.

When a supernova occurs, clouds of material are blasted out into space. This stardust makes up the ingredients that will, one day, form new stars.

About 340 years ago, there was a supernova in the Milky Way. Hubble Telescope images show a massive ring of material moving at speeds of up to 31 million miles an hour (50 million km/h) away from the explosion. The glowing cloud of gas and dust is known as Cassiopeia A.

That's Out of This World!

As a supernova occurs, a massive shock wave creates temperatures in the star of tens of billions of degrees Fahrenheit (Celsius). These extreme temperatures can create **elements**, such as gold or plutonium, from the material that was once the star. These elements are then thrown out into space.

Fast-moving clouds of supernova leftovers

Cassiopeia A

THE CRAB NEBULA

On July 4, 1054, a huge, bright light appeared in the sky. The mysterious light, witnessed and recorded by early astronomers in China, was a supernova.

Today, the remains of this supernova are known as the Crab Nebula.

An image created by the Hubble Telescope shows a massive gas cloud that is still expanding out into space from the original supernova explosion. The cloud, or nebula, is expanding at about 930 miles per second (1,500 km/s). The nebula is made up of supernova leftovers and now has a diameter of around 11 light years!

At the center of the cloud are the remains of the giant star—a star that was, in its lifetime, 10 times the mass of our Sun.

That's Out of This World!

The 1054 supernova could be seen in the sky during the daytime for about three weeks. It was visible at night for up to two years.

The Crab Nebula

A Very Important Nebula

Sun

When old stars die, their remains become the ingredients for making new stars and planets in the future. About five billion years ago, gases and particles of dust from long-dead stars and supernova explosions were floating in a nebula.

Part of the cloud began to collapse on itself. Dust and gas collected, creating a massive ball, or sphere. As the sphere rotated, or turned, in space, a disk formed around the sphere from the remaining gas and dust. As all this matter spun, more gas was drawn in, and the sphere ignited to become a star—our Sun! Leftover matter from the formation of our Sun clumped together to become the planets of our solar system and their moons.

The chemical ingredients for our Sun, the Moon, our Earth, and everything on our Earth—even those that make up you—were once floating in a beautiful nebula!

That's Out of This World!

The gases that make up nebulae include hydrogen, helium, oxygen, and nitrogen. The particles of dust might be rock, carbon, iron, or nickel, or a mixture of these. Most of the dust particles are so small you would need a microscope to see them.

Earth

Recycling Stars

The Sun is about halfway through its life. In about five billion years, as its supply of fuel runs out, our Sun will begin to die.

In the final stages of its life, the Sun will grow bigger and bigger and become a red giant. As it swells in size, the Sun will swallow up Mercury and then Venus. Eventually, our planet will come to a fiery end as our star swallows up the Earth.

When the Sun's life finally comes to an end, it will begin to blow off layers of material out into space. Ultimately, it will become a white dwarf star surrounded by a planetary nebula.

Material that was once our Sun, our Earth, and everything on Earth, will be floating in a nebula, ready to become the ingredients to make new stars and possibly new worlds!

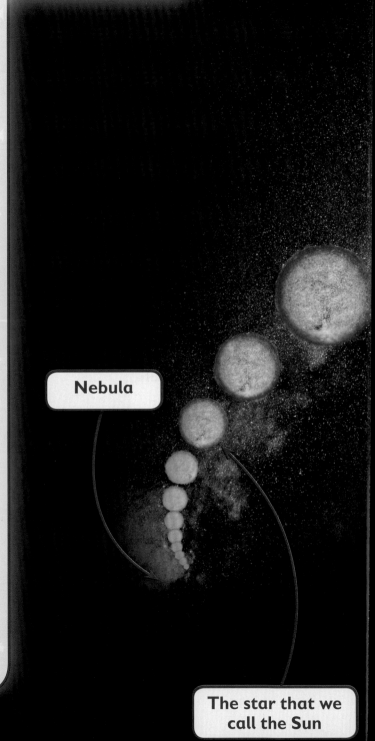

Nebula

The star that we call the Sun

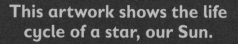

The Sun becomes a red giant

A planetary nebula

That's Out of This World!

When the Sun swells to become a red giant, its diameter will grow by 250 times!

GLOSSARY

astronomers (uh-STRAH-nuh-merz)
Scientists who specialize in the study of outer space.

atmosphere (AT-muh-sfeer)
The layer of gases surrounding a planet, moon, or star.

elements (EH-luh-ments)
Pure chemical substances that are found in nature. Hydrogen and helium are the most abundant elements in the universe, and iron is the most abundant element making up planet Earth.

galaxy (GA-lik-see) A group of stars, dust, gas, and other objects held together in outer space by gravity.

gravity (GRA-vuh-tee) The force that causes objects to be attracted toward Earth's center or toward other physical bodies in space, such as stars or planets.

Hubble Space Telescope
(HUH-bul SPAYS TEL-uh-skohp)
A telescope that has been orbiting Earth since 1990. Its pictures of the deepest reaches of the universe are far superior to anything viewed from a telescope on Earth.

light year (LYT YIR) The distance light can travel in a year—more than 5.8 trillion miles (9.4 trillion km).

Milky Way (MIL-Kee WAY)
The galaxy that includes Earth and the rest of our Sun's solar system. The Milky Way is believed to contain around 400 billion stars.

nebula (NEH-byuh-luh) A massive cloud of gas and dust in outer space. Many nebulae are formed by the collapse of stars, releasing matter that may, over millions or billions of years, clump together to form new stars.

orbit (OR-bit) To circle in a curved path around another object.

red giant (RED JY-ant) A star that is nearing the end of its life cycle. As it uses up its energy, it grows in size and the temperature of its outer atmosphere begins to cool off, giving it a reddish-orange color.

red supergiants
(RED SOO-per-jy-intz) Stars that are far larger in terms of size and volume than any others in the universe as they near the end of their life cycle.

solar system (SOH-ler SIS-tem)
The Sun and everything that orbits around it, including asteroids, meteoroids, comets, and the planets and their moons.

sulfur (SUL-fur) A pale yellow, nonmetallic chemical element that is one of the most common in the universe. It is used in the making of gunpowder and is found within massive stars.

supernova (soo-per-NOH-vuh)
A super-bright explosion of a star that creates a sudden release of energy and light. Its remains may form nebulae.

white dwarf (WYT DWARF)
A small, very dense star at the end of its life cycle that has thrown off most of its outer material, creating a planetary nebula around it and leaving only the hot core of the star burning brightly at the center.

WEBSITES

For web resources related to the subject of this book, go to: www.windmillbooks.com/weblinks and select this book's title.

READ MORE

Aguilar, David. *Super Stars: The Biggest, Hottest, Brightest, Most Explosive Stars in the Milky Way.* Des Moines, IA: National Geographic Children's Books, 2010.

Fleisher, Paul. *The Big Bang.* Great Ideas of Science. Minneapolis, MN: Twenty-First Century Books, 2006.

Miller, Ron. *Seven Wonders Beyond the Solar System.* Minneapolis, MN: Twenty-First Century Books, 2011.

INDEX

A
absorption nebulae, 14
astronomers, 12, 14, 16, 19–20, 24
atmosphere, 5

B
Barnard, E. E., 19
Barnard's Merope Nebula, 19

C
Calabash Nebula, 20–21
Carina Nebula, 10–11
Cassiopeia A, 22–23
Cat's Eye Nebula, 20
Chandra X-ray Observatory, 10
Crab Nebula, 24–25

D
dark nebulae, 14
diffuse nebulae, 10

E
Eagle Nebula, 4
Earth, 4–5, 8, 10, 12, 14, 18, 20, 26–28
emission nebula, 10, 16

G
galaxy, 10
gases, 4–7, 10–12, 14, 16, 18, 20, 22, 24, 26–27
gold, 22
gravity, 6

H
Horsehead Nebula, 14–15
Hubble Space Telescope, 5, 7, 10–14, 19, 22, 24

L
light years, 8, 12, 14, 18, 20, 24

M
Mercury, 28
Merope, 18–19
Milky Way, the, 10, 22
Moon, the, 26

N
NASA (National Aeronautics and Space Administration), 14
nebulae, 4–8, 10, 16, 18, 24, 26–28

O
Omega Nebula, 8–9
Orion Nebula, 6, 8, 12–13

P
planetary nebulae, 20, 28–29
planets, 12, 20, 26
Pleiades, 18
plutonium, 22

R
red giants, 20, 28–29
red supergiants, 22
reflection nebulae, 16–18

S
Seven Sisters, 18–19
Sigma Orionis, 14
solar system, 8, 26
Sun, 5–6, 8, 16, 20, 22, 24, 26, 28–29
supernovas, 6, 22–24, 26

W
white dwarf star, 7, 20, 28